An Uncommon Life

An Uncommon Life

MOID U AHMAD

PARTRIDGE
A Penguin Random House Company

To order additional copies of this book, contact
Partridge India
000 800 10062 62
orders.india@partridgepublishing.com

www.partridgepublishing.com/india

Dedicated to my parents

Prologue

Suhanto was going to his office along the busy roads of Delhi, moving swiftly under the influence of a red beacon. Momentarily he looked outside the car and visualized a glimpse of a particular moment to which he could relate. He noticed that one family of four was waiting to cross the road which included a man holding hand of a girl of about four years along with his wife who was carrying a boy of about one year in arms. This sight instantly reminded him of his past and it appeared to him that it was his family he had just visualized. There were tears in his eyes. It often happens that when someone is contended with ones achievement and looking back at the not so good past always brings out tears. These tears are probably influenced by sympathy for someone and for someone it may be influenced by conscience or maybe because of some other reason but one thing is for sure that these tears are because of some pure emotions, something to which one can relate and something which is buried deep in the heart which becomes explicit because of some particular incident or scenario.

Suhanto was the governor of the central bank of the country, one of the coveted roles which any finance professional strives for. He was a happily married man with a caring wife and a talented daughter and belonged to a farmer parents who still reside in the village. He has grown from being a rustic village boy to a clever banking professional but still is very much connected to his roots.

1

Suhanto was born to a middle class farmer family in a 'not so remote' village Pallanpur in one of the 'better off' districts of the state of Uttar Pradesh in Northern part of India. As the poverty line varies across geographies, there are economic categories of people in rural and urban areas. A middle class farmer in a village can be thought of as someone who grows and sells vegetable and manages to save something on daily basis. This means that the family has to constantly grow, reap and sell vegetables throughout the year by following short crop seasons for seasonal vegetables. Suhanto, as a child used to accompany his father to the field and to the market since he was five years old. Initially it was more because of fun and excitement which later on became a routine because of the need for more working hands to support the family. Suhanto was the only son along with an elder sister, four years elder to him. His mother belonged to a nearby village, Chappur, and was the only child of her parents. The family of four was living decently in their modest earnings and was living like any other farmer family often facing the 'life' tests which are common in rural areas in India.

The state of Uttar Pradesh is one of the largest state of the country in terms of population and geographical area and sends the maximum number of representatives to the Parliament. The state holds great political importance and thus is the cynosure of all political parties of the country. It has tremendous economic potential but lacks in industrialization in comparison to other prosperous states of the country.

Summers in a north Indian village are pleasant in the early morning and in late evening hours. The major threat to living comfort is mosquitoes and humidity. Additionally, the 'hide and seek' playing electricity supply often makes the situation worse in summers. Although the supply has improved and villages can expect few hours of electricity supply in the night, even though at low voltages but still manages to provide psychological comfort to the dwellers. The voltage at most of times is so poor that the light from a 100 watt electric bulb feels shy of the light spread from a good candle. If the weather is pleasant in a village, it can be traded for any extravagant comfort of the rich. A *pleasant breeze in a village is like a fresh lease of life*. It is extremely soothing and touches everyone like a touch of a loved one.

As Suhanto used to accompany his father, Manikka, to the field, he had learnt the art of sowing, nurturing and reaping by burning his fingers under the sun. This 'three step process' of farming is one of the simplest production process, bolstered by nature, and teaches one of the essential lessons of life but most of the people involved do not understand the gravity of this process. Manikka owned one 'Kachha Bigha' of land on the outskirts of the village where he used to juggle between crops such as potato, tomotao, gram and peas as common vegetable to grow for sale as well for consumption. Often if circumstances were favorable, he used to grow 'pepper mint' as a cash crop. One 'Kachha Bigha' is one third of 'Pakka Bigha' which equals to about 3000 square yards. Suhanto as a child enjoyed a lot being in the fields. Helping his father in cultivation using a pair of bullocks or spraying pesticides or at the time of harvesting, enjoying the fresh peas and grams and sometimes having them as roasted was the earnings of the day.

Every season in a village has its uniqueness. The Sun sets early in winters and one common tool to fight winter cold is to light fire by using the abundant organic things available in villages varying from dry sticks, wood from trees, dry stems and even 'Kanda', which is an innovation on cow dung, a very popular and common fuel item in villages. Somebody has to just ignite the fire, commonly known as 'Alao' in local jargon and suddenly there is flurry of people joining in to feast on the heat, often bringing in something as their fuel contribution to the fire. This result in a social gathering around the fire and people just cuddle up irrespective of cast, creed and religion. Someone in jovial mood may start singing in the local dialect or someone more stoical would feast on the heat and contemplate. Often people manage to arrange for some eateries by contributing and sharing peanuts and other items over discussions. Roasted potatoes, grams and peas are common delicacies during winters in villages. Using the omnipresent fire, in the 'fire clubs', the members often roast these commonly available crop items such as potatoes, sweet potatoes and peas and feasted on the freshly baked products.

Suhanto remembers one very humorous incident during one such gathering. One common attire for male villagers is 'Dhoti' or 'Lungi' or 'Thaymad' which is a long cloth which covers the lower part on their body. Once 'Ajannu Chacha', aged, bored and boring soul of the village, was so engrossed in criticizing the local politician that he did not realized that his 'Thaymad' had come in contact with the fire and was heating up. The folks, who noticed, wanted him to go away and so it happened and no one warned him. Suddenly Ajannu Chacha was running with his burning attire which during his run had to be taken off and he was ultimately running without it. He was lucky that it was dark and absence of electricity had helped him to get away without being embarrassed. Everyone laughed their heart out that night and the incident was in news for quite some time in the village. Next time when Ajannu Chancha joined a different gathering he made sure that he was aware of his garment and that he did not criticized anyone.

The discussions during these winter gatherings varied from topics like crops to new 'Nautanki' in town. Seniors in the gathering always gave suggestions and often unwanted to new generation on crop issues and human life in general. But the discussions were always on the lighter side and everyone took the discussion in the right spirit. 'Nautanki' was another common topic of discussion. It refers to the moving drama caravans, performing in villages and primarily in local dialect. The performances by these moving drama clubs were one of the most after sought activities in the villages. These drama troupes were often called by the rich of the villages on occasion of celebrations to provide some entertainment to the villagers and express their gratitude. These were primarily sponsored events and the sponsors used to take the front seats, near the stage and everyone else would sit on the ground on first come, first serve basis. Thus, always there was rush to occupy a place near the stage. Since the troupe had few female members, the performances always had a 'natural' demand. The troupe usually did a short duration drama which included few latest movie songs. Being a sponsored event, the monetary reward from the spectators was the icing on the cake for the troupe. Often people, especially boys in the flash of excitement, used to stand up, dance or pass comments, which resulted in hooting and shouting and ultimately silence had to be maintained by the self made 'bouncers'. It so happened once that during one of the performance which depicted a dance performance in a bar from one of the gangster movies, one adolescent boy, stood up, flashed a handmade crude pistol and started dancing to the tune of the song. Suddenly there was hustle in the gathering and the play had to be stopped for few minutes to remove the boy from the place and calm down the spectators. It was always exciting in these events. Suhanto used to attend these shows with his father and later along with his friends but his mother always wanted him to refrain from attending them as she felt these would distract him to a wrong path often citing the example of 'Babloo', a village boy, who had eloped with one of the female performers. Occasionally these drama events were informative also. Suhanto still remembers few lessons on patriotism, honesty, hard work from some of the performers.

Suhanto used to go to a village school which was about two kilometers from the main village and was named 'Convented School'. This was the first private school in the neighborhood. The name probably was influenced from the concept of 'Convent' schools of the urban areas which were considered to be benchmark in quality education. Although this school was no way near quality education and the only things similar was the name, still the promoters of this school projected quality education as value to stakeholders and thought that it would be a good business model. The school ultimately became famous not for its education but for the grey areas in delivery of education. It came to be known for its 'Yum' and 'Yal' which actually indicates the pronunciation for alphabet 'M' and 'L'. It was a boy's school, as expected in a rural area. On his daily walk towards the school, Suhanto had to pass through the government sponsored school of the village where the resounding voice of students chanting numerical tables and trying to mug them up was a daily sight. The shouting of *'doo ekkum doo, doo dooni chaar'* and likewise always could be heard from a long distance. Suhanto always used to wonder whether there is any difference in learning style in both the schools and always contemplated that which school was a better learning platform. He has witnessed students from this government sponsored school to excel and move to good schools in the city.

Khanta was a boy, two years senior to Suhanto, whom he considered as his best friend. They used to stroll together to school. Sometimes Khanta would bring his father's bicycle along and Suhanto used to sit on the rod provided in the front part of the bicycle whereas Khanta used to ride. This was the typical 'masculine' bicycle available in villages which served various purposes from ferrying three people together to carrying sacks of grains or load of vegetables. Whenever bicycle was available, both Suhanto and Khanta used to visit nearby places to enjoy. Even just a ride on a bicycle was a luxury and entertainment at that point of time. The popular game of the village was 'Gilli Danda' which was a mix of golf, baseball and cricket although cricket as a popular game was fast catching up with the entry of solid plastic balls.

The monotonous and simple life of a village was filled with colours and joy on the occasions of various festivals. Pallanpur was a village with people from mixed caste and different religious beliefs. Eid, Bakra-Eid, Muharrum, Holi and Diwali were few prominent festivals celebrated in the village. One of the common items of rejoicing was the 'mela' or fete organized on these occasions. Different types of swings, rudimentary toy shops, local eateries and shops selling daily items were few of the attractions in these gatherings. Also it was the time for the mono colored life of village boys to become colorful by providing them an opportunity to scout for romantic partners.

The village environment is usually cordial to all. The pace is slow and everyone has lot of time to spend. The people are simple and generally have concern for one another. One very significant and differentiating factor between a village and a city is that in a village everyone has a sense of collective responsibility towards things and issues.

In this kind of simple village environment, Suhanto was brought up and thus had built a strong character which he believed would certainly help him in future. Unlike other village boys, he was different, he wanted to be different and he was not shy of taking responsibilities.

2

Chimpi and Suhanto were about the same age. Suhanto never tried to find the exact age of Chimpi, but he surely knew that her birthday falls on 23rd April of every year. Chimpi and Suhanto were neighbors. They first met at the age of seven at Suhanto's home. It was recently that Chimpi's mother had made her visit to Suhanto's house more frequent maybe because of Chimpi's proximity to Suhanto's sister. This was a blessing in disguise as Suhanto also made a friend and these three had lots of fun together. Chimpi's father owned a small sweet's shop in the village market and thus Chimpi always brought some eateries with herself in every visit and everyone relished on these sweets. They used to play traditional outdoor games like 'Pakram-Pakrai' and 'Gitti Phor'. The first game is like catching a thief and the second one is like hitting a pile of stones with a ball and running to avoid being hit from the same ball. Then there were traditional indoor games like 'Chirya Ud' and 'Kana Phoosi', the former played in a group and one needs to differentiate between flying and non flying things as the names of the things are called. The second game involved whispering in each other ears and then laughing if 'Tomato' became 'Potato'. In summers during day, most of the games had to be indoor and at night outdoors, often in dim light of a lamp.

Very soon Chimpi and Suhanto became good friends. They were in the same class although in different schools. Suhanto went to 'Convented School' while Chimpi went to the government school in the village. Chimpi's father never wanted her to go to school but because of persistent effort of Chimpi's mother, he conceded and got her admitted in the school. Chimpi was an average student where as Suhanto was the better of the two. They often discussed syllabus and other classroom stuff. Suhanto was very good in mathematics and thus Chimpi had the privilege of a private mathematics tutor as friend. Chimpi and Suhanto had a great time together in the village. They used to go to mango orchards in summers and relished on juicy mangoes and played 'Lachhi Chum', a game in which one had to climb trees, jump on the ground, kiss a stick and climb back without getting caught. During winters favorite games were jumping on the stacks of used rice shafts or cycling. During rainy season one common game was building bridges for ants and making paper boats.

Gradually time passed and as they grew old, the closeness of two children gradually converted into affection and they started missing each other when they were not together. They liked the sensation when accidently they touched each other while playing. *They knew they liked this and they also knew that the other person knows this.* They liked each other's company. Often they would visit the neighborhood mango orchard and sit their quietly gazing at the sky and listen to birds chirping. Since people were used to seeing them together all the time, probably no one objected to their friendship.

Chimpi passed her high school with second division and Suhanto passed with first division and came third in the village. At that time first division was considered good and percentages were not much in state boards. Even people used to treat a 'high second division' as good. Suhanto's family was very happy as he was the first in the family to pass high school with first division. He received good amount of money as reward which he quietly deposited in his piggy bank. The two most important gifts to him were given by his sister and Chimpi, both of them gifted a pen each.

Suhanto's sister got married when he was in high school. His brother in law had a garments shop in the nearby village and was the only son in the family. The local pundit had brought the proposal initially which had finally materialized after few meetings amongst the two families. Suhanto and Khanta enjoyed a lot in the marriage. It was an occasion for them when they had ample opportunities to relish on eateries of various types and often unlimited. Amongst all the hustle and bustle of the marriage, somewhere in his heart he had this feeling of loneliness and separation. It was good that Chimpi was at his side for consolation and share his sadness. The day his sister went to her new home, Suhanto did not ate for one whole day. It was suddenly that he had lost his appetite and taste for eateries which he had been enjoying for few days. Gradually he got busy in the admission process for intermediate course and made few rounds to the city with Khanta to scout for admission in a good and affordable college.

As Chimpi passed high school, her parents actively started to look for a groom for her. Chimpi has grown as a beautiful young lady, tanned in complexion but with a very bright face and sharp features. Although there were few marriage proposals for her from the village itself but they were not found fit for Chimpi by her parents and family. The local matchmaker also tried to connect few families but somehow things could not worked out. Chimpi's parents had saved some money for her marriage but they did not wanted her to get her married only using money. Chimpi's paternal aunt, who lived in Delhi, finally brought a proposal which seemed attractive to all. The boy's name was Naresh and he helped his father in the business of manufacturing steel pipes. He was ten years elder to Chimpi but her parents agreed because they knew that at young age even if difference is high, things work well. Of course the age difference between Chimpi's parents was twelve years.

Chimpi got married to Naresh and shifted to Delhi. Suhanto was studying in the Pallanpur city and he had managed to take out some time to visit Pallanpur village for Chimpi's marriage. He was quite involved in the marriage preparations like any good neighbor and was available day and night to offer best comfort to the groom's family on behalf of Chimpi's family. Suhanto's and Chimpi's families had been very close to each other and it was the time to celebrate and participate. It was like a family affair for Suhanto and his sister, who had also arrived especially for the marriage. The marriage was solemnized at a decent scale which included a number of popular traditions and customs. In villages, usually marriages are conducted during daytime. A 'Nautanki' was also organized on the eve of the marriage. The whole ceremonial process was a three day long event and finally the 'Vidai' took place on the third day. One bus and three cars had accompanied the procession or 'baraat' back.

That night Suhanto had cried. It was because of happiness or grief, he was not sure, but he was sure that he felt a vacuum around him, some sort of a gap, a feeling that something has permanently gone. After staying back for another day, he came back to the city and joined his school and gradually got comfort in the company of his friends.

3

Suhanto moved to the city to pursue higher studies. He took admission in government Intermediate college as tuitions fees was manageable there. He shifted in a private place nearby the college and shared a room with four other students. It was a makeshift hostel in the vicinity of the college, managed by a wealthy family by converting one of their ancestral property into a hostel. Initially Suhanto did not liked the place but gradually he became comfortable and became used to the daily routines. He had to get up early, get ready, eat something outside and reach college by 7:30 am. Then come back from school and keep busy with the studies. The five boy's living together belonged to the same district but different villages. They were Mohan, Rakesh, Khaleeq and Raju, apart from Suhanto himself and all of them had somewhat distinct aspiration. Suhanto and Mohan wanted to join a government job but Suhanto was more ambitious of the two. Rakesh and Khaleeq somehow were skeptical about government job. In fact they loathed the work environment of government offices. They were more influenced by west and dreamt of going abroad. Khaleeq was more enterprising and risk taking of the two roommates. The fifth, Raju wanted to do his own business. He was very casual with studies but had sharp business acumen. Since they were all in the same section of the college, they shared many things in common and gradually they became a close group which was known as 'Panjee' in school. During festivals they took breaks to visit their places and on returning shared the delicious eateries they brought with themselves. Occasionally they went to watch movies or roam around the market place. All of them believed in the philosophy *'All work and no play makes Pappu a dull boy'*. It was a group of simple village boys, unadulterated by urban culture and focused on their dreams.

Cricket was one common hobby they shared. Weekends were usually busy playing cricket matches. Raju was the most prolific all round cricketer in the group. They had tried to build a team by joining hands with school mates and then participated in cricket tournaments.

Time passed by and their friendship became stronger. They all had worked hard for their intermediate exams and finally came the eve when result was to be declared. The result was published in the evening edition of the local newspaper. Since the newspaper was in demand and everyone was excited to see the result first, the newspaper was usually sold at a premium price. A one rupee newspaper may sell at twenty rupees. Most of the students would wait, holding their breath, for the newspaper vendor to appear with newspaper on bicycle. There used to be a huge gathering of students at different road crossings across the city waiting for the result.

That evening they had waited for six hours when finally the newspaper vendor appeared on bicycle with one newspaper in hand and shouting *'Inter ka result, bees rupiah mein'*. Quickly few students joined hands, collected twenty rupees and purchased the newspaper from the vendor. All of the five friends had cleared their intermediate exams. Suhanto, Rakesh and Khaleeq passed with first division while Mohan and Raju passed with 'good second' division.

They celebrated that night by going to a movie.

Life moved on for 'Panjee'. They moved from college to university.

The first division holders and even Mohan managed to join the preferred course in the 'City University' while Raju had to be contended with whatever course was available. Four of them got admission in the coveted Bachelor of Science course with Computer Science, Statistics and Mathematics as subjects while Raju took admission in Bachelor of Arts (BA) programme. Since all of them were friends and were fortunate to get admission in same university, they planned to stay together and rented a house in a nearby locality. Suhanto and Khaleeq started to give tuitions to school children and managed to earn some money to improve their standard of living. The other three managed to negotiate with their families for increased monthly expenses. Now once a month they could afford to eat a lavish meal at a good place or buy a new shirt. They also contributed money to buy a portable black and white television, the specific purpose of which was to watch cricket matches.

One of the advantages of staying together in college days is that one can fend off the upcoming dangers and conflicts with a show of unity. Once Khaleeq had some argument with a classmate over his proximity to a girl and he was thrashed by other suitors of the girl. Suhanto and Raju managed to reach on time, put up a fight and rescue Khaleeq. Later, a compromise was reached upon by intervention from few senior students.

The 'Panjee' was quite popular in the university and they had managed to build a reputation amongst other students.

Suhanto and Mohan joined a Bank Probationary Officer's (PO) coaching centre. At that point of time while Rakesh and Khaleeq were a bit casual as they were sure that they would be doing a Master of Science (MSc) course and then go for a doctorate course (PhD) abroad. Suhanto and Mohan knew that they need to work hard to qualify the highly competitive bank exams and took their studies very seriously. Often when electricity was not available, they used oil lamps and sat on terraces for group study but tried not to skip practicing questions and problems. Suhanto and Mohan formed a prolific pair and usually studied together. The other three friends may have not taken studies seriously but they were also smart brains. Persistence was common to all five.

Time passed. All of them cleared their graduation with first division. Rakesh and Khaleeq got admission in MSc (Computer Science) in Hyderabad University and had to join at the earliest. Suhanto and Mohan cleared the written PO entrance examination for Diamond bank and had to travel to Delhi for interviews. Raju had to go back to his village to help his family in the family business and thus he was the first to leave. All five friends were at the bus station to see off and say good bye to Raju. It was a busy travel season and busses were overflowing with passengers. Raju somehow managed to get some place to stand in a bus with luggage being ferried on the roof top of the bus. It was a short journey of two hours and thus could be managed, even standing. Raju was known as a jovial person in the lot of five. Although he was sad on this separation, he pretended to be in jovial mood. For the last five years they had been living like a family. There was bound to be a void in their lives after this separation.

Rakesh and Khaleeq were next to leave the group. It was another emotional moment for the group when they got together at the railway station to say good bye to Rakesh and Khaleeq. One consolation was that all of the friends were on the right career track. While coming back from railway station Suhanto and Mohan hardly spoke to each other for a day. Gradually they came out of the phase of silence and loneliness and started preparing for their interview in Delhi. They still had few days to leave and they wanted to give their full focus to the effort.

Suhanto and Mohan had come to Delhi for the first time. In fact, it was their first visit to a metropolitan city. They were mesmerized to see the size and scale of development in the city. They booked a room in a small lodge in the 'Paharganj' area of the city and stayed back doing the last moment preparation. The interview was scheduled next day in a government office in the 'Connaught Place' area of the city. Suhanto's interview was satisfactory but Mohan did well in the interview, answering most of the technical questions. After the interview they went on to roam around the lovely places across the city, starting from 'Connaught Place' itself. They stayed for another day to visit historical monuments like 'Lotus temple' and 'Qutub Minar'.

The interview result for the PO job in Diamond bank was declared after two months.

On a bright morning Suhanto was awakened by a violent trembling of his body. It was Mohan. He had a copy of 'Employment News' in his hand and a wide grin on his face.

'Get awake, you have been successful in the PO interview. Your name is here in the list of selected candidates.'

Initially Suhanto thought that Mohan is joking but when he saw his name in the list, he could not believe it. His interview was not very good and he was not very optimistic and hopeful about a favorable result. Somehow it seemed like a dream come true as he dreamt of a government job. Suddenly he felt alleviated and tension free. Suddenly there was this momentary feeling of calm and he felt relaxed. Very quickly he came back to reality. He looked at Mohan with a curious face.

'No, my name is not there in the list', Mohan spoke with a heavy heart.

Suhanto was happy and sad at the same moment. He was glad because of his selection and lucky to have a friend who could be happy in his happiness and was sad that such a friend was not selected. He was speechless and wondered what to say to Mohan. Never the less they celebrated this moment and kept on discussing the reason for selection or non selection. Suhanto called his village and communicated this message to his parents using a 'PP phone'. A 'PP phone' is a phone set which is owned by a neighbor or nearby shop keeper and which can be used to take calls or messages, usually for emergencies.

Suhanto had to join his job in two months and meanwhile needed to do the paper work. He also wanted to go home but did not wanted to leave Mohan alone at this juncture. Mohan understood this and finally decided that he will go back to his village as of now, comeback later on and keep trying for other PO examinations.

Mohan and Suhanto spend the next few days in winding up their five years setup in the city. Lots needed to be done as Raju, Rakesh and Khaleeq had left most of their belongings behind and something needed to be done about them also. They sold the television to one of the fellow students, sold some of the text books in the seconds book market, sold the three bicycles and other home appliances and from the money received, paid of the two months pending rent to the landlord and gave him a notice to vacate the house. Suhanto also had to serve a notice to the students whom he gave tuitions and he received some arrears from them also.

Finally the day came when the two remaining members also had to part ways. They both decided to keep in touch and took different bus to their villages, saying good bye to the city which had given them friends, confidence and education to do well in life ahead.

4

Khaleeq and Rakesh joined the Master of Science (MSc) course in Hyderabad University. They were fortunate to be in the same university and thus stayed together but now they have become a much closed group, keeping up to themselves and interaction with others was usually professional in nature. They became more focused in studies, living up to their dream of going abroad and preparing themselves accordingly. Even they had managed to get their passport ready just in case things get expedited. They lived in the university hostel and shared a room. Khaleeq continued giving tuitions and he convinced Rakesh to take them also. Now they tutored higher classes and could earn better. Both of them were very fond of non vegetarian food and often took time out from their schedule to relish on the delicious Hyderabadi Biryani. Occasionally they managed to speak to other friends or exchanged letters.

Suhanto joined Diamond Bank and became busy with his life in the bank. He had joined in the head office of the bank and had managed to find a place of dwelling in a nearby residential area. He used to commute using a bus which took hardly fifteen minutes to office. He felt alone and tried to manage his loneliness by spending more time in the office. Often he could spend time using the rich library of the bank. He had become more focused on his professional life and wanted to do good and big in his career.

After about a year of their separation, Mohan wrote to other four friends about his selection in 'IOU bank' and that he had to join in a branch in Mumbai. This was good news for all friends. Everyone was very pleased, particularly Suhanto, as he was worried for Mohan when he could not get through Diamond bank with him and also because since other friends had moved ahead, he may feel dejected and frustrated. The news of Mohan's selection came as a big relief to him.

Meanwhile Raju had joined his family business of rice and flour mill and he had shared that now he is planning to expand his business outside the village and maybe visit Delhi, Mumbai or Hyderabad to scout for new business opportunities.

The entire five friends were now moving on their chosen path. They were probably lucky or may be their bonding and friendship had provided them with opportunity and confidence to face the competitive world. There was a sense of satisfaction amongst all as everyone was satisfied with themselves. This was indeed a true example of bonding and strong empathy.

5

Rakesh and Khaleeq got learning opportunities abroad to pursue Doctor of Philosophy (PhD) program. Khaleeq was first to get a call from a university in America and Rakesh after few months, from a university in Germany. They were to be separated by continents. They decided to go as they thought that a local degree is the opening door to their career in a foreign country. Also considering the fact that a PhD degree is a good learning opportunity in computer sciences and that they were to receive scholarships and work on some breakthrough technology. It seemed to be a rationale decision to go abroad for higher education and exploit the opportunity.

Khaleeq had to leave at short notice. He just managed to make a short visit to his village and meet his parents. He had a talk with Suhanto, Mohan and Raju on phone. It was very painful for him to say goodbye to Rakesh. They had been a family for seven years and especially those seven years which involved adult and adolescent phases of life. In fact they had grown together and passed some of the critical phase of their life in each other's company. Rakesh bid adieu to one of his close associate with teary eyes at the airport. These tears were of joy and separation, both.

Few weeks later, Rakesh also left for Germany.

Both, Khaleeq and Rakesh were from a middle class background. Although they had managed to save some money from their tuition earnings, but still had to arrange additional money to fund the onwards flight and some amount to cover the living expenses for initial few months.

Khaleeq was very quick to adapt to the western culture. He took up a part time job during his studies. Although he was receiving a scholarship but being somewhat ambitious he decided to use the available spare time to accumulate some savings. His performance in studies was satisfactory and being an extrovert person, very soon he was able to build lucrative contacts and extend his personal network. He had a good physique and was decently good looking. He used to play cricket and quickly adapted to playing baseball. He became quite popular in his university and very soon he was more American than Indian, at least apparently. He completed his PhD in about three years and took up a job in a software company in the Silicon Valley. Khaleeq married an American citizen, Julia, during his PhD and he kept this as a secret from everyone. Only Rakesh was aware about this secret.

When Khaleeq came back to India after two year of job, he disclosed the secret about his marriage to his family and it was a scene to watch. He had informed his family that he is coming with a female friend which was something not common in a village. His mother could realize and exclaimed *'he is coming with a girl; I have a bad feeling about this!'*

Khaleeq reached his village with Julia. He witnessed that it is a moment of celebration there. Then he realized that he was the first person from the village who had gone to America and now he is coming back after a gap of five years. It was like a case of someone lost was found. Also, it was a matter of pride for the entire village. People were waiting with garlands in hand to meet Khaleeq and maybe get a glimpse of his 'Angrezi' or foreigner friend. It was a tough task acknowledging all the people gathered at his home. He had never expected this type of grand welcome as he had been living an ordinary life in America. He thought to himself that this could happen only in India.

It was at night, post dinner, when most of the family members were together, Khaleeq decided to disclose his secret. He announced *'I have to tell something'*.

'My friend Julia, is actually my wife. We married two years ago'.

'Kya'!

'What are you saying?'!

'Yes, this is true. I wanted to tell at the time of marriage, but then I thought that I would inform personally and give clarification about the situation. She had agreed to convert to Islam and changed her name as Ruksana'

Surprisingly everyone took the announcement in right spirit and behaved in a mature way as if they were expecting this news. Of course there was no other option other than to accept as they had been married for two years. Khaleeq later on explained the circumstances to his mother separately that Ruksana is a good girl, they both liked each other and are living happily.

His father went one step ahead and announced *'Since we could not attend the marriage we would surely host a feast for our relatives and friends in the village itself'*.

The marriage feast and the stay in an Indian village was a different experience for Ruksana and she enjoyed every moment of their short trip. She always wanted to visit India particularly, rural India, and she was not disappointed. She never imagined that her visit would be in connection to her marriage. She enjoyed a lot. After staying back for a fortnight, they returned to America. While coming back from the village, they had managed to take a brief detour to visit 'The Taj Mahal' at Agra.

On the other side of the Atlantic Ocean, in Germany, Rakesh was busy with his teaching and research.

Rakesh's initial stay in Germany was not as easy as Khaleeq's. When he had reached Germany, he had a difficult time while adjusting to local language and culture. Even food was a big issue which was very different in taste and material. Gradually he settled down and started working on his research with full dedication and determination. He managed his expense in the little scholarship he received and was on the campus for almost 24 hours, everyday, focusing on his studies. He had managed to get a hostel nearby to his department to save on travelling time. His efforts gave him dividends. In the first year itself he won the best research scholar award and repeated the feat in the second year. By the end of third year he had published around ten research papers in good journals. Based on his publication record and research contribution, he was awarded the Doctor of Philosophy degree in the third year itself.

After passing out from the university he took up a teaching job in a graduate college in Frankfurt. Next year he came back to India, got married and went back with his wife.

Raju was the only friend who could attend the marriage and it seemed that he was the common reference point for the five friends.

While Khaleeq and Rakesh were galloping ahead in the west in their professional and personal life, Raju in a small village in India was planning business strategy for his business. After coming back from the city, Raju joined his family business of rice and flour mill. Although his family was doing a decent business and was one of the wealthy families of the village, Raju somehow was not contended with this routine business. He wanted to expand and grow the business. He was the youngest of four children and was very enterprising.

Raju had probably decided his future career while he was in the university and he had gradually started working on his business acumen. Probably this was the reason that he was a bit casual with his studies. He had tried to understand the dynamics of business purely because of his interest. He had subscribed to a business newspaper which he read very religiously while his other friends loathed this 'pale colored' newspaper. He used to interact with small businessmen like tea stall owners and tried to understand their model of doing business. Often he also used to attend the business seminars and conferences organized in the city by industry associations and academic institutions. He had gradually understood the art of doing business by his sporadic but persistent efforts and now he wanted to apply his learning's. Raju's family business was managed by his elder brother, who was also a graduate but was more contended with whatever he was doing and was not ambitious. Raju discussed his plans during one of the interactions over dinner. He used to call his father as 'bapu'

'Raju, now since you are back after your studies, it is expected that you join hands in the family business'. Raju's father addressed him.

'yes bapu, I am also thinking on the same lines but I think that we are doing things in a very routine way and if we could changed the way we do our business, we can grow business by a good size. As I have estimated that the average revenue of the business is growing @10% per annum and if we try to expand we can surely grow at double this rate'.

Everyone was baffled and astonished at this statement. They were not used to such type of business discussion and that too over dinner.

'Raju, your thoughts are good to ear but can it be done?'

'Also from where would we get money for expansion?', Raju's brother raised eyebrows.

'I am confident that it can be done and we will try to arrange money somehow but first we need to be in unison that we need to expand'

'But Raju, don't you think that we are doing well and it is sufficient for our family?', Raju's father expressed his apprehension.

'Father, it is good that we are doing well but if we do not expand we will stay behind in competition. Allow me some time to understand the business and market in detail and then I can be more specific in answering the queries'

His father agreed to give some time to Raju to prepare and then reflect on his thoughts. Raju spend the next few days understanding the market of his village, nearby village, even the city market for rice and flour. He also scouted for modern and more efficient machines available for his business. His survey revealed that in the urban areas there are people who are willing to pay a premium for a better quality and healthy rice and flour and the existing market price in the city is almost double of the price at which he sells in his village. Also he found out that in the village there is a large segment which is price conscious and would buy more at less price.

Raju discussed this with his father and brother and proposed that if they try to sell their products in the urban market they can increase the margins and subsequently can use the byproducts to sell at a low price in their village and the nearby villages. He also shared that there is one machine available at a price of three lakh rupees which can be used for producing flour and which can also be used for processing and polishing rice. He proposed that in order to increase the production capacity of the existing business they can buy this machine by taking a loan from bank. His confidence and seriousness was very apparent and his father conceded to his proposal, although to be implemented in stages. His brother was apprehensive initially but on further explanation he also got convinced.

In coming months Raju was very busy with his plans. He bargained a loan deal at favorable covenants with a public sector bank and purchased the required machinery and got it installed on a vacant piece of land on the existing factory compound. He hired a diploma engineer to operate the machinery along with other labor. Initially the production work was moved on to the new machinery as it was more efficient and if load was above capacity it was shifted to the old machinery. Raju has already done contracts (not legal but in the form of promises) with village farmers that the farmers would be selling their produce to Raju which would be further processed and sold in villages and the city. Thus he was assured of continuous supply of raw material and the farmers were also happy that now they do not need to go to the local market to sell their produce. Raju knew that in order to sell his products in the urban market he needs to do good packaging and he will require a brand name. He named his brand as 'Dharti' and also set up a small packaging unit. He had formally tied up with few wholesalers in the city and sold the 'nicely packaged' flour and rice under the brand 'Dharti' to them. The remains of processed rice and products which could not be sold in urban markets were sold in villages at low price to those who wanted them. Thus he was able to sell in city at more margins and he was able to sell all the remaining stuff in local market at low margins but at high units of sale which also converted into some profits.

His father and brother used to manage production and he looked after marketing and other operational issues. The business model promoted by Raju was a huge success initially and his brand 'Dharti' became famous in nearby villages. Soon he expanded to three new plants in three year and his product started selling very well in the city also. Now he was ready for the next round of expansion into far off cities like Delhi and Mumbai.

At the same point of time at different places, Khaleleq and Rakesh were busy with their studies, Suhanto got married and Mohan was doing well in 'IOU' bank.

6

Suhanto was very excited on his first day at work when he joined Diamond Bank. He wore a nice blue cotton shirt with contrasting trousers and was feeling smart. He got a joining in the head office of the bank, a twenty storey building in the heart of the city. He was given a cubicle, a telephone connection and a personal computer to work with. His immediate reporting boss was one gentleman by the name Prateek and he had to meet him formally to discuss his job and role. After completing the joining documentation process in the human resource department, the administrative officer of the bank showed him the way to his cubicle and wished him good luck. Suhanto sat on the chair with a sense of pride and satisfaction. Very few people from his village were working in government job. In retrospection, he could feel the sense of achievement. Coming from a very modest and rustic background, he had struggled and somehow managed to get into a good bank at a decent job profile. He could have been contented by this achievement but there was something which encouraged him to go for more. Maybe his habit of putting extra effort in everything to counter his economic and social disadvantage was putting steam in his engine. Or maybe the attitude which he had developed, working in the fields, in his village was making him to work even harder. When a farmer is working in a field, he is not sure about the outcome of his efforts in the form of crop but still with an expectation of good result he does not wants to leave any stone unturned in his effort.

The first call from his desk he made to his mother. It was a 'PP' number which is referred to as *'Padosi ka Phone'* or neighbor's phone or sometimes as *'Pass ka phone'* but eventually indicated a telephone connection nearby which can be accessed.

'Amma this is Suhanto calling from Dilli'.
'I have joined the bank and calling from office desk'.

His mother was very glad and started crying with joy. In her shivering voice she said *'I always pray for your good. God bless'*

After disconnecting the phone Suhanto kept on thinking that how proud her mother would have been and she would be now boasting of her son's achievement as he was the only one in his immediate family from maternal and paternal side who joined a government service. He also tries to recall that once one of his distant relative passed a comment that Suhanto is incapable of doing anything good in life. He thought to call that relative and inform that person that this incapable boy has been found capable by the government. Somehow, he refrained by making that call, thinking that such comments are passed casually by people who are not able to do anything significant in life and subsequently these people try to be contended by humiliating others. He can easily recall numerous incidents where senior people in his village very casually used to pass judgments on juniors like *'Tumse zindagi mein kuch nahi hoga'* (You cannot do anything in life) or '*Tum Bewakoof ho*' (you are a fool). With his very little experience of life, Suhanto can confidently conclude at this stage that every person has some natural talent and if he/she is allowed to explore things under limited guidance, he/she can do wonders in life.

As Suhanto was going through the hurricane of thoughts, past and present, suddenly the phone on his desk rang.

He picked up the phone.

'*Hi Suhanto. This is Prateek, your boss. Can we meet?*'

Suhanto replied in affirmative and stood up to leave. He knocked on Prateek's cabin door and request permission to enter.

This was the first formal meeting between Suhanto and Prateek.

Prateek was a middle aged man, around 45 years old, well built and smart looking. They shook hands and Prateek signaled Suhanto to sit down.

'*How has been your day? How do you feel?*' Prateek questioned.

'*Sir, it is an honour to be part of such reputed name and to be working under such an able manager like you. I have joined, gone through the documentation process and ready for the job*'.

'*Good that you have joined. I feel flattered from your words but I hope this is not the way you work*'.

'*No sir, certainly not*'. Suhanto answered. '*I am more of a doer kind of person*'.

'*So what are your expectations from the bank in terms of job profile*'.

'*Sir, I look forward to do something challenging and technical as I want to develop a skill set which is difficult to replace*'.

'That is good. So how about being a part of the credit division of the bank looking after Industrial loans'. Prateek proposed.

'Perfectly all right sir. I think I needed some role like this. So how do I start?'

'Straight away, take this file and let me know your decision that whether we should fund this project or not?' Prateek signaled towards a file kept on his table.

Suhanto picked up the file from Prateek table, went to this table and started reading the file. He was shocked to read the name of the applicant, Naresh. Immediately he verified the details and his fear was found to be true. Naresh was the same person who had married his childhood love, Chimpi, and was a person with high ego. Suhanto did not liked him personally for 'obvious' reasons but also Naresh did not seemed a good human being to him. This person was a businessman based in Delhi and has been married to Chimpi for few years. Subsequently Suhanto tried to connect the dots that Chimpi had moved to Delhi after marriage and since her husband's business was also based in Delhi, he had applied for a loan with this bank.

Gradually Suhanto moved from personal domain to professional domain in his thought process. On having a glance at the file it seemed that the loan proposal was not worth the five crore loan requested. Naresh's business was incurring losses and it was not a very convincing case for loan approval. Suhanto was caught in dilemma between his heart and mind. Technically, the project would not be approved. The business was in dire need of funds and he wanted to help Naresh for the sake of his lost love but if funded, there was a high chance that the bank would incur loss on this account. The first professional task given to him should be a success else it would effect his career prospects. He was confused and uncertain. His mind was facing a turbulence of thoughts. He could not believe the intention and motive of destiny behind this coincidence and situation.

He thought, how small was the world?

Should he discuss this situation with Prateek? Maybe this will not give a good first impression.

Should he get in touch with Chimpi and discuss with her without informing her husband?

Should he recommend funding on this loss making, highly risky proposal?

Should he behave like a true banker and act like a true professional?

He was unsure. He wanted to give more time to himself on this situation.

It was almost lunch time. He decided to distract his mind and wanted to take a break from these thoughts and got up for lunch. Being the head office of the bank, it had a centralized canteen where food was available at a subsidized rate. Reaching the canteen he found that his boss Prateek is having lunch at a table with few other seniors. He wanted to avoid Prateek so as to avoid questions on the loan project. At times it happens that one runs from problem and finds that the problem is chasing him or her. Prateek saw him and signaled him to join in.

'Hi, it is your first day and lunch is on me. Although it is a modest lunch, do please order anything you like'. Prateek asked Suhanto.

Suhanto was not feeling hungry and so he ordered a plate of 'Rajma' with rice.

'So did you managed to go through the loan proposal?' Prateek asked the inevitable question.

'Not in detail. I am on it. When do you need me to finish?'

'One week'. Prateek replied spontaneously.

Suhanto felt relieved that he has some time to his advantage and by the time he will surely think of some win-win solution to this complex 'personally professional' problem.

Post lunch, Suhanto decided to stroll around the place and maybe approach the problem with a relaxed state of mind. The bank was located in posh area of the city in a large commercial centre which also had a small street market. He walked through the area and was trying to assimilate the air, environment and ambience into his thoughts. After all he will be in this place for few years at least and it is better to get familiar with the place.

Somewhere in a deep corner of his heart he felt excited. Destiny has given him another opportunity to be near his lady love and probably meet her. During these few years he had hardly met Chimpi and was excited. Gradually he was making up his mind that he needs to help her by helping her husband. This thought gave him joy and a soothing feeling. He returned to office and started going through the proposal again. Now he was thinking on his 'modus operandi' to get the project funded and saving his reputation also. Maybe this required to take calculated risk. He was learning fast and he learned a lot on his first day.

The next day Suhanto made a call to Naresh's office and came to know that he is out of town for few days. He sensed an opportunity. He straight away called Naresh's house and to his surprise it was picked up Chimpi. Although the voice sounded different on telephone but he can recognize the accent of her voice in thousand voices.

Suhanto had to gather his courage to speak.

'Main bol raha hoon'

There was a deep silence on the other end of the telephone. This meant that she had recognized his voice also.

'How did you get this number?' Chimpi was surprised.

'You can call it destiny'. Suhanto replied.

'What do you mean?' Chimpi was still puzzled.

'I have joined Diamond Bank. The loan application submitted by your husband is being considered by my office'.

'Ok'.

There was a long pause in the communication.

'I want to meet you. Can we meet somewhere?' Suhanto asked hesitantly.

'I do not know'.

'Ok. I will call you again in the evening at 5pm just to check'.

Suhanto disconnected the phone, relieved at his achievement. He had heard Chimpi's voice in many years.

The remaining part of the day was a long day for Suhanto. It seemed that the clock had stopped and 5 pm seemed too distant. Suhanto called Chimpi at sharp 5 pm and they agreed to meet next day at a restaurant at 11 am.

Next day Suhanto reached his office a bit early, made an impression in the office that he was very busy in work. Although physically he was in office, mentally he was somewhere else. He informed his boss that he is going out and left the office around 10 am.

Chimpi arrived early at the restaurant. Suhanto reached right on time. She was sitting on a corner table and the moment Suhanto entered they caught a glance of each other. A gap of few years seemed a gap of many years. Two people, once very close to each other, behaved like strangers. Maybe because both of them had moved on in life in different directions. Both of them had a lot to share but tried to keep calm. They wanted to share each other's excitement but they realized that they are in a public place and things have changed. Excitement was abundant in their conversation. They interacted for about two hours, sharing their past with each other and then subsequently realized that they both are living a very distinct and separate life. She was happily married and he was busy with his career. Chimpi mentioned that although her husband's business was doing good, it has incurred huge losses in recent past. Suhanto indicated that the loan proposal revealed all these details. He also shared the dilemma which he was facing and that the loan proposal had very narrow chance of being approved with any of the bank. Chimpi suggested that he should take a professional view of the situation and not base his judgment on emotions. Suhanto replied *'Let me see what can be done'*.

They left in about two hours. Chimpi drove in her husband's car while Suhanto took an auto rickshaw. They promised to keep in touch and meet soon. During the discussion, Suhanto had finally made his mind. He was going to help Chimpi's husband. He had to somehow manage the loan proposal.

Over the weekend Suhanto kept on thinking and working on loan proposal. He did two things. One, he changed the financial statements attached in the file indicating profitable business and secondly, he modified few statements like cash budget to indicate healthy financials in future. By Monday he was ready with a very impressive loan proposal. He shared his 'modified' view with his boss and consequently the loan was cleared for funding. Suhanto had managed things in a way that Chimpi's husband would never come to know about his role but he was sure that Chimpi would understand his decision and action.

7

Time passed. Suhanto gradually became busy with his job. He met Chimpi occasionly without the knowledge of Chimpi's husband and both understood each other's situation. His boss, Prateek, was very happy with his work and his dedication to the job. Prateek occasionally invited him to his house for dinner. Prateek's sister, Pinki, lived with him and she was doing her MBA from a private management institute. She liked Suhanto and this was very apparent in the way she talked to him. This was noticed by Prateek and he tacitly approved of this relationship, although he was unsure whether Suhanto reciprocated her feelings or not. He wanted to discuss this with Suhanto and was waiting for the right moment which, incidentally he got on the occasion of Pinki's birthday.

It was a small gathering and Suhanto was also invited. He took along a book as a present for Pinki.

While the party was on, Prateek took Suhanto to a corner for a chat.

'Do you like partying?', Prateek asked Suhanto.

'No, not exactly. My upbringing has been in a very modest and traditional background where such gatherings do not exist'.

'Yes, I understand. But I think now you should be used to such parties as they would be a routine activity in your lifestyle'.

'Yes, maybe'. Suhanto nodded.

'What are your future plans, like marriage and all, you know?' Prateek was gradually coming to the point.

Suhanto immediately sensed the motive behind this question.

'Sir, I have not decided yet. I have to buy a house first, shift my family here and maybe then I would think about it'. Suhanto gave a very frank and precise reply.

'Ok. Let me know when your parents are in town. It would be a pleasure to meet them. Enjoy the party'. Prateek left Suhanto, relieved that he had made his point.

About three years of joining the Diamond bank, things worked well between Suhanto and Prateek and after few rounds of meeting between Prateek and Suhanto's parents things were getting settled. Suhanto and Pinki also managed to meet at few occasions and understand each other. Suhanto finally agreed to marry Pinki. During this time period, using his savings and taking a subsidized loan from bank, Suhanto had managed to buy a small flat at some distance from the bank. At the time of marriage, Prateek offered to buy him a bigger flat but he politely refused and even refrained from taking anything in cash or kind as dowry. Also he made it very clear to Pinki and Prateek that he was from a modest background and his style and standard of living may not be similar to Pinki's style of living and that Pinki will have to adjust accordingly.

His parents were very happy with this alliance. The marriage took place during summers in Delhi but one lunch was to be organized in Suhanto's native village, Pallanpur, for his near and dear relatives who could not attend his marriage in Delhi. The marriage was a very closed group affair, attended by immediate family members from Suhanto's side. He had met Chimpi, few days prior to his marriage but refrained from inviting her as it could have disclosed the loan proposal issue and maybe Chimpi's husband could have known about their clandestine meetings. Also, to keep Prateek out from the loop, regarding Suhanto's role in Naresh's loan process. Out of Suhanto's four friends only Raju could attend as others were busy at that point of time.

The marriage lunch at the village was a major event during Suhanto's marriage. His parents, Pinki, Prateek and he himself reached Pallanpur one day before the lunch. As usual there was an electricity cut which is more common during summers. During these years, Suhanto had invested some money in his village house and renovated it. Also the neighbors were ready to offer their houses to guests if required. The stay of guest was managed but the summer heat was unbearable. Amongst all this arrangement, lunch was also to be managed. Sunahto's sister had arrived early and she took the responsibility of managing things initially along with her husband Shailu. Suhanto on his arrival took charge of event management. The lunch was to be arranged in an open ground in the village which usually was used to host the local bazaar. The menu was a decent vegetarian menu and was prepared by the famous cook of the village who otherwise was very busy but on the request of Suhanto's father, agreed to offer his services. Suhanto's father could not do much on his daughter's marriage thus he had planned to fill up all the gaps and invite most of the villagers and relatives. It was a sort of 'open to all' lunch. Buffet system was used and the food being tasty was liked by everyone. It so happened that for once there was a flurry of guests and the 'Naan', a local variant of bread went short. There was a long queue of people waiting for 'Naans' with plates in hands which finally was controlled after a gap of half an hour. It was a very anxious moment for all. Simultaneously, there were lot of traditional events and songs going on inside the house and Suhanto had to keep shuttling between attending guests outside and meeting his commitments inside the house. Pinki enjoyed these events a lot. Everything finally went off well. Prateek was also very happy and he along with Suhanto and Pinki returned on the next day to Delhi.

Pinki had also adjusted effectively in the new home. She was liked by all, particularly by Suhanto's parents and this aspect of the new relationship made Suhanto felt contended and glad.

8

Suhanto's life was on a growth trajectory, personally as well as professionally. His sister was happily married, his parents were enjoying their living in Pallanpur and he was now also married happily. He was doing well in his job and his other four friends were also more or less settled in their career. He used to send money regularly to his parents to so that they do not need to work anymore. In fact, he and Pinki had requested them to accompany them to Delhi but somehow they were reluctant to leave the 'habitual' comfort of the village for the sake of a new life in a new city. His father had answered *'It is very difficult to leave in this age'*.

Suhanto could understand that his father has spend his all life in building networks and relationships in the village and now his life is an imperative part of Pallanpur.

After a year of his marriage Suhanto was promoted to Senior Manager and transferred to Hyderabad. He was repenting that if this would have been earlier he could have spent some time with his friends Khaleeq and Rakesh. By this time both of them have left Hyderabad to pursue their careers abroad. Khaleeq had gone to USA and Rakesh went to Germany.

Since Suhanto's new role involved a lot of travel initially and also because he had to make stay arrangements, he went alone, leaving Pinki to stay with her brother.

Suhanto had to travel to villages and rural area of the state, meet with customers, study the market and use all the data collected from primary sources for decision making. Once he went to a village to scout for reasons for increasing loan defaults from borrowers of that particular village. He came to know that most of these borrowers were cotton farmers and the crop has been destroyed by pests for the last two years. These farmers having no other source of income, borrowed more money to buy food and defaulted on the loan because of non availability of revenues from crops. He was sad to learn that few farmers had committed suicide also because of increasing debt and lost respect and more over to avail government's compensation for their families. Although he had seen poverty during his life in his village but this was a superlative effect of poverty he had witnessed. Also he was more depressed as he could relate to the life of farmers very closely.

Suhanto came back to his office, determined to find a solution to the suicide problem. This issue was worrying him personally as well as professionally. The suicides were eating up the fund base of the bank and diminished future prospects of banking business. He also felt a moral responsibility towards the farmers as a banker and as a human being.

On carefully analyzing the situation he found out that the situation needs to be dealt at various levels. At the initial level the bank needs to relook at the lending norms and recovery processes and at other level the bank should work in coordination with farmer groups to provide technical support for primary and alternative employment to enable the farmers with continuous income. Suhanto prepared a proposal and presented it passionately to his seniors. The senior management of bank was very impressed with Suhanto's proposal and accepted it straight and full. Also he was made the 'officer in charge' of the whole state to implement this program which was termed as 'Banker friend' program of the bank. It took around one year to make the program reach majority of the target farmers. As expected the program was successfully implemented and the response was favorable. The bank had managed to reduce suicide rate and increased loan recovery. Suhanto was awarded for this successful scheme by a promotion and was transferred back to the head office at Delhi as *Assistant General Manager (AGM)-Strategy*. It was not common in a bank that someone had received a promotion so quickly. Suhanto and Prateek were now at the same level in the bank. Of course, Prateek was very happy for Suhanto and Pinki, not only because of the personal relation but also because Suhanto was once his disciple and it always brings a sense of satisfaction to witness the students grow.

Coming back to the head office as AGM-Strategy, Suhanto implemented a number of prolific initiatives in the bank regarding product development, pricing and business expansion. Soon he became a popular and respected soul in the galleries of the head office of the bank.

Suhanto was also progressing well on the personal front. Within a year of coming back, he was blessed with a beautiful daughter. Both Suhanto and Pinki were very excited. On this occasion Suhanto's parents also got an opportunity to spend some time with them in Delhi. Suhanto's father proposed the name 'Rupali' for the girl and was liked by all.

Suhanto kept on moving on deputation to different parts of the country although he managed to keep these assignments short as he did not wanted to unsettle his family. Rupali had a joined a good public school in Delhi. Suhanto always tried to contribute something different in each of these assignments he took. This was the reason that he always got respect and appreciation when he left the place. He kept on getting regular and frequent promotions and became the Managing Director of Diamond bank at the age of 46, the youngest in the history of the bank.

9

On one evening in February, Suhanto was working late in office and the phone on his desk ranged at around 7:00 pm. He picked up the phone.

'Mr. Suhanto?'

'Yes'. Suhanto replied.

'This is Khan, personal assistant to the Finance Minister of India'

Suhanto had met Mr Khan, a couple of times on official matters.

'Sir, how are you?'

'I am fine Mr. Suhanto, the minister wanted to meet you'.

'Right sir, when and what time?'

'Will coming Friday, 5:00 pm would be fine, at his office'

'Sure'. Suhanto confirmed.

'Ok then let us meet on Friday'

Mr Khan hanged the phone. Suhanto was not very sure about the purpose but he was sure that there must be something important if Finance Minister has asked for him.

Suhanto left office and reached home. Rupali and Pinki were waiting for him.

'What took you so long?'

'This Delhi traffic is becoming worse day by day. Anyway what is the plan?'

'The repeat telecast of the Oscar ceremony is on'.

'Ok, how about a cup of tea?'.

'Sure, Ramu kaka, please bring tea for Sahib'

'Please I am no Sahib'

'Ok, Ok, how was the office?'

'The finance minister wants to see me on Friday, I am not sure about the reason'

'Great, these meetings are always for good'

'Maybe, let us see'. Suhanto expressed his apprehension.

The next few days were usual in office but Suhanto was trying to find a clue about the meeting with Finance Minister so that he may be better prepared for the meeting. His preliminary enquiry revealed that his name is being considered for the post of the governor of the central bank. Although he was not sure about the reason, he was still preparing for the meeting considering he was offered the 'coveted' job.

Suhanto had discussed this with his wife and daughter and they had wished him good luck on the day of the meeting with the Finance Minister.

The day did not started well as he had to reprimand one of his juniors for delaying an important project finance proposal. Suhanto very rarely lost his cool and today was one of those unfortunate days.

Rest of the day was as usual and he left his office at four pm to reach the FM's office on time. Luckily at this point of time, the traffic was comfortable and he reached 15 minutes ahead of the scheduled meeting. While he was interacting with Mr. Khan, they were called up to meet the minister.

Suhanto had met the Finance Minister once in a private party. He was a handsome man with sound credentials as a politician as well as an economist.

Mr Khan introduced Suhanto to the minister and left.

'Minister Sir, Mr Suhanto is here'

'Good evening sir'. Suhanto offered his greetings and offered to shake hands with the minister.

'Good evening Mr. Suhanto, it is a pleasure to meet you, how are you?

'I am fine Sir, how are you?'

'Oh, the usual political and economical problems'

'Sir, you take care of the politics and let the bankers take care of the economy'. Suhanto made a statement on a lighter note.

'Sure, I like this confidence and good sense of humour, both of them very critical at this level and perhaps this is the reason that we are meeting'

'Mr Suhanto, you have established your name as a banker and the best thing is that you have a clean career.

Minister further added. *'You must be aware that the current governor of the central bank is about to retire in few months and we are considering a number of names for a successor and you are one of them'*

'Many thanks for the honor, it was least expected'

'I hope you do not have any apprehension about the same'

'No, infact I look forward to it'

After spending about 30 minutes with the Finance Minister, discussing various topics, Suhanto returned home and shared the news with his family. All were very excited.

After few more round of discussion with the Finance minister, other ministers and even one brief meeting with the

Prime Minister, it was finally announced that Mr Suhanto would be the next governor of the central bank.

Suhanto was a busy man that day. Till late evening he was on phone accepting good wishes for his new role. Personally he had mixed feeling. He was feeling happy and responsible. It was a moment of celebration at his home. His parents could not understand the meaning of governor and he had to explain that it is the biggest post in banking in the country and that his name would be there on the currency notes. It was then they realized that this is something big and eventually his mother started crying with joy over phone. In the same way the message was passed on in his village and he later learned that there was a huge celebration at his house in the village.

Suhanto's farewell party at Diamond bank was high on emotions. He had spent about 30 years at the bank and grew in the ranks from a trainee officer to Managing Director of the bank. The bank was a school as well as a bread earner for him. He had learnt almost everything during his experiences in the bank and this was the prime reason that the farewell was very emotional for him. Almost every staff member from the head office was present. He had already sent a message to everyone that no gifts are expected but still few employees were bold enough to bring something for him. His farewell speech was very emotional thanking every employee, starting from a peon to the Chairman of the bank. The party went till late night and finally Suhanto and his family managed to reach home at four am in the morning. Luckily next day was a Sunday and he could afford to take some rest amongst the highly busy schedule of his in recent times.

10

About a week after his farewell from Diamond bank, he joined as the governor of central bank. His family was present along with a host of politicians, economist, bureaucrats and people from media.

Suhanto's first speech as the governor of central bank was very much appreciated.

'My dear colleagues. It is an honor and privilege to be a part of this esteemed organization and getting an opportunity to contribute my bit as its governor.

I thank each and everyone who has been directly or indirectly connected to me.'

He then went on to underline other issues along with his priorities and focus area in his new role. In his speech, Suhanto had made it very clear that he wanted a transparent and efficient system in the central bank. Suhanto was not a hard task master but always took his job seriously and the same he expected from his team.

Suhanto's first day at office went into many introductions with his secretary, support staff, deputy governor, other subordinates and many others. There were three deputy governors under him and he had an informal meeting with them over lunch discussing points and issues varying from current economic scenario to international markets to political equations.

Amongst the few prominent roles that the governor of a central bank had to perform are controlling liquidity in the economy, controlling inflation and ensuring economic stability in the economy. Apart from keeping a close eye on the economy the governor had to maintain an amicable relation with the ruling government as often there are conflicts over policy and philosophy. It took few days to Suhanto to understand these dynamics and then he moved on to develop his action plan considering all the prevailing parameters.

The central bank has to review the monetary policy at least once in three months. Few days earlier to such a review, Suhanto called a meeting of the board of the central bank for discussion on the same.

'I thank you all for coming for this discussion meeting and I welcome you'

'As you all are aware that very soon we are going to review our monetary policy and we would be discussing this, however, I must bring out one important consideration for our discussion'

'Recently I had a meeting with the honorable prime minister and he had raised his concern about high and rising inflation. Although we as a super regulator need to take decision based on logic and rationale but we need to respect the concern of the executive, which maybe politically motivated. On the other hand, inflation is our primary concern too, at this moment. Thus we have to focus on the monetary policy with an objective of inflation targeting. Now, the house is open for discussion'

Mr Pandey, one of the board members spoke: '*The economic data suggests that inflation is rising because of increasing demand of consumer goods. We need to curb this demand and somehow provide for additional supply of consumer goods, which may bring down the prices.*'

'*It is a valid point*'. Suhanto added.

Dr. Verma, another board member raised his concern about the rising import price of crude oil and its effect on inflation.

The brainstorming meeting went on for six hours and finally some consensus emerged.

In the subsequent monetary policy announcement, Suhanto announced an increased in lending rates. The decision was applauded by most, with few being skeptical but ultimately the policy had affected in reducing inflation.

Some of the good decisions and some not so good but logical decisions improved upon the popularity graph of Suhanto and gradually he became a well respected figure amongst the political class also and particularly he became a close associate of the honorable Prime Minster (PM) who used to consult him on important policy matters.

In one of the government's meeting, in which Suhanto was an invitee member, and chaired by the PM, an important issue of rural development was being discussed. Suhanto was very inclined to attend this meeting as he always was interested in making his contribution to such a cause. The meeting started by the PM giving the opening remark and raising his concern about the slow and unorganized growth of rural regions of the country. The minister for Rural Development raised an important issue that we have made sound plans for the rural sector, we have required funds also but there are issues with implementation. Even if we assume that some funds dry up before they are used for the intended purpose, still the issue of effective implementation remains. There was lot of deliberation and talk on the issue during which Suhanto also gave his inputs on the same.

'Considering the concern of the rural development minister regarding the implementation issues I can very confidently say, of course based on my experiences of the rural areas, that in most of the cases intention to implement is present but the person responsible for the implementation needs proper advice and guidance or we should say a second opinion and if that is provided, things can improve. I had tried to implement a process known as 'Banker Friend' during my experiences with farmers at my previous bank and I should state that it was very successful. In that programme, the loan officers were also playing the role of a mentor to the borrowers apart from doing their regular duty. Although this exactly cannot be implemented on this issue which we are discussing but certainly a modified form of it can be used for effective rural developments schemes.

I propose that a mentoring programme should be initiated by the rural ministry where retired officers of the government can be reached to become 'mentors'. These 'mentors' would be working in the areas where they are currently residing and they would be requested to join on 'purely voluntary basis'. There would be no fixed payment made for the service as it would be voluntary. However they can claim certain miscellaneous expenses to a limit. They would be primarily advising and suggesting the district magistrate on development issues in the rural sector of the district. I am sure that we can find around 500 volunteers who would be willing to join the cause. If this scheme is implemented, please consider my name as a volunteer.'

The PM lauded the thoughts of Suhanto and felt a sense of consensus emerging on this proposed scheme. Also three other officers sitting in the meeting nominated themselves as the mentors. It was not clear to Suhanto whether these officers gave their name to come in the limelight or they were genuinely interested. The PM also liked the scheme and requested the rural development ministry to prepare a policy document on this 'Mentoring programme'.

11

It was on the day of marriage of his daughter, Suhanto learned about the demise of Chimpi. She passed away in the same morning and was survived by a son and a daughter. Since the funeral was in Delhi, Suhanto could manage some time to attend the cremation. He had a strange feeling that moment. He lost one of his most affectionate associate on a day which probably was the happiest day of his life.

Suhanto's daughter Rupali's marriage was an arranged one. The groom was an investment banker and working in New York. A friend in Suhanto's office had played cupid. The best part of the marriage was that all the five friends were to assemble together for the first time after they were separated on passing out from university. All of them had made advance plans with sufficient time at their disposal.

Khaleeq came with his wife Ruksana, a son and a daughter.

Rakesh came with his only son as his wife had passed away few years ago due to cervical cancer.

Mohan and wife came along. They had an adopted daughter, Stuti.

Raju came along with his wife and four children. His brother in law and family also accompanied them. Khaleeq was currently associated with a software company as its Managing Director, owned a large house and was doing good in California. Rakesh had gradually grown in academics and was currently serving as Dean in a good university in Germany. Mohan was quite contended with a stable banking job and was still with 'IOU' bank at a senior level.

The marriage was to be solemnized in the Delhi Convention Centre, which was providing for the stay arrangements also. It was a premium venue and thus had to be booked in advance and Suhanto had to use some influence to get the venue booked for the marriage.

The best of arrangements and lavish menu was served. The who's who of the banking and finance domain were present. It was ornamented by the presence of VVIPs. The Prime Minister was also expected to attend but could not make it finally because of a last minute change of plans. He was represented by the finance minister.

However for Suhanto the major attraction was reunion of friends. Even their families were meeting for the time, all together.

They had planned a visit to the village and to other places which connected them and were of common interest. Once they were free with the marriage, they decided to take a tour to Pallan pur and their village.

All the five friends decided to give something back to the society, especially to the school where they first met. They decided that they would establish a 'charitable trust' which would be looking after the charitable initiative of the friends. They planned a visit to their school. The Principal of the school, Dr. Sharma was a very approachable person. He gladly requested them to visit the school at a date and time of their convenience and even offered to arrange an interaction with the students for them. However they turned down the offer of the interaction as they wanted to keep their visit a less known affair.

Dr. Sharma initially gave them a brief about the latest developments and achievements of the school.

'We have been doing well in high school and intermediate exams. Few of our students go to good universities and colleges. However, we are facing acute shortage of funds to maintain the infrastructure and cover operational expenses and thus unwillingly had to raise fees'

'This is unwanted, how would a poor guy study if he cannot afford fees?', said Suhanto.

'I think we need to do something', said Mohan and looked towards other four friends. He could see the acknowledgement and approval of the proposal he had in mind. They knew each other.

'Can we propose some scholarships for students?', asked Mohan.

'Of course you can do, why not?'. The principal replied.

'Okay, I am sure that my friends would agree, we propose five fully funded scholarships for top five students in terms of high school marks who take admission in intermediate course and this would cover all tuition and living expenses for two years. Also this scholarship would be announced every year'.

'It is perfectly fine' said Suhanto and others nodded.

'It would be a great news for the students and a shot in the arm for the employees', exclaimed Dr Sharma.

It was decided that either Raju or Suhanto would do the formalities and the scholarship would be available for the upcoming session.

After the school visit, they went to the same old building where they used to live together. The building was there, the room was there but the surroundings had become more populated and polluted. The building was also in bad shape. They learnt that the owner had died and the building was now looked after by his son who was more inclined in selling the building rather than running it as a private hostel for the school students. They discussed amongst themselves that if the owner is willing they can think of buying the building and convert it into a charitable hostel for school students which would be managed by a trust.

Luckily things worked out and later on they purchased the building where they had lived, renovated it, formed a trust by the name 'Shiksha Educational Trust (SET), which would maintain it. Initial contribution of one crore was made by all five friends. It would be used for maintaining the hostel and scholarships for initial three years.

On one of the days they decided to visit the City University. It was a Sunday and they had the luxury to roam amidst the silence of the university corridors and enjoy some moments of privacy. The classroom, the canteen, the ageless banyan tree, the cycle stand, playground and many other places. It seemed that it was just yesterday they were studying and then realized that almost 35 years have passed. It was a lovely evening they had at their leisure. In fact there were tears in Rakesh's eyes, recalling the good old times.

12

Suhanto journey back to the village was not an easy one. Just like his journey out of the village, which itself was not easy.

The government's mentorship program was an ambitious project. Under this program the government had tried to rope in retired government employees with significant contribution in the respective fields as advisor to the local government/administrator. The role was given purely on voluntary basis and was purely an advisor role. In terms of monetary payouts, only the actual travels and certain miscellaneous expenses to a limit were to be reimbursed.

Suhanto had opted to become the mentor at his native district and thus he was required to advise the District Magistrate of the district on issues related to administrative and implementation of policy. The DM office was required to invite and inform Suhanto about any pertinent meeting and he may or may not attend. It was expected that at least four such meetings should be attended in a year by the mentor.

Suhanto had an option to stay in the city (he had purchased a flat there) but he wanted to stay in the village to be closer to his field of operations. Although mentoring was a voluntary job, he took it very seriously as he wanted to give something back to the village. Another reason for the same was that his parents were living in the village and he knew that they are in the last leg of their life and he wanted to be with them as he had missed their presence all along his life when he had left village. He was 60 years old when he retired after serving for two terms as the governor of the central bank. His father was 85 and mother around eighty years old. He came to know about the exact date of birth of his parents very late only when he was in diamond bank and he had applied for passport for his parents. He was surprised to know that even his parents were not very sure about their date of birth and the reason which they gave was very strange. They told him that at that point of time there was no tradition of keeping records of birth and the village chief simply issued a certificate of birth and whatever one could recall was recorded as date of birth.

Suhanto's parents were glad that their son was staying with them. They already had built a house at the time of Suhanto's marriage and with some minor repairs and modification it was ready for his 'comfortable stay'. Suhanto had refused to get the air conditioner installed there but had to relent on the persistence of Pinki and eventually had to install the required power backup also. Even the people at Pallanpur were rejoicing at the arrival of Suhanto as most of them perceived that some big personality would be staying in their village and that their village will now have some favorable inclination of the district administration. Suhanto had a very clear agenda in hand regarding his future course of action. He had decided that he will spend the first few years very seriously on the mentorship programme and maybe then pass on the baton to someone else. He had also informed the coordination body about this time line.

Suhanto spend first few days relaxing and enjoying the silent and cool ambience of the village. Summers was approaching. He could sense it in the air as he felt the same odour in the air which otherwise could be termed as pungent. He noticed that not much has changed in the village since he left except few concrete constructions, less dense green cover and some modern days machines such as mobiles and automobiles. He used to read these developments on paper in his reports earlier and now he can witness the changes. Surely things have changed in villages but the change is sporadic. He could find that few families who were poor previously are still poor and few families, who were more enterprising and risk taking have accumulated a lot of wealth.

Suhanto wanted to first understand the issues before he could suggest or advice anything to the administration. Initially, he informally used to interact with villagers to get inputs and then verify the same from his father. His mother also often presented a different, tacit perspective of the women folks and their problems in village. Subsequently Suhanto requested for a meeting of the village 'Panchyat', the local managing body of the village, to share his views and discuss issues with the villagers.

Suhanto's first meeting as a mentor was quite a learning for him as well for the people present. It was presided by the District Magistrate and other senior officials of the district were present.

The District Magistrate (DM) opened the meeting, *'Some of the larger problems in villages are health and farm related issues. We urgently need to tackle the problems in hand'*

The DM's secretary, Mr Babu, rubbing his big belly interrupted, *'but sahib these issues have been there since long and we have schemes for all these problem but people do not come forward to use these services'*

'Mr Babu, Let us discuss the issues and we would request your input wherever required', the DM interrupted Mr Babu

The DM seemed to be a wise man although just few years in civil services.

Suhanto, *'please let us know the gaps and the available resources, then only we can suggest some action plan'*

'Mr Babu, please present the data to all on available resources, deficiencies and focus areas', the DM instructed the secretary.

During Mr Babu's presentation it was apparent that there are bigger issues of resources and implementation.

'Sir, we should address each of the issues one by one and then in due course maybe try to leverage some of the existing network and resources', Suhanto made a point.

Some of the people in the meeting were not used to such strong jargon for discussion and they tried to understand as much they can. It was brought forth that the district has four medical ambulances allotted by the health ministry for the rural areas but they were not being used frequently and were underutilized, especially in comparison to the number of births taking place in the district. Analyzing the relevant data, Suhanto thought of one solution.

'DM sir, I would suggest that we should be proactive, get the pregnant ladies registered, calculate the expected date of delivery

and make the ambulances available even if the patient does not asks for. Since currently all the four ambulances are based in the city, we need to decentralize the bases, divide the district in four geographical section and allocate one ambulance to each section. Decentralization would surely help'.

The suggestion was quite helpful and when implemented, increased the utilization of ambulances. After the initial meeting, the DM was very impressed with Suhanto's contribution and always looked up to Suhanto for suggestions and advice. Often he personally visited Pallanpur to interact and discussed issues with Suhanto. Suhanto enjoyed his stay in the village. The first year passed successfully for Suhanto in his role as a mentor and some of the suggestions he gave to the district administration were very helpful.

Suhanto's mother was not keeping well and he was lucky to spend some quality time at leisure with her. His mother often used to say she was happy to see his growth and now she has no regrets in life and she can die at ease. His sister who was married in nearby village, often visited and it used to be a good family time.

Suhanto's mother passed away in the third year of his coming back to Pallanpur. He missed her but was mature enough to understand the ultimate truth of life, which is death and which every living being has to face.

He spent another one year after that, finished his assignment as a mentor and returned to Delhi where also he had a house and where he had spend most of his life. He tried to convince his father to accompany him but again he was unsuccessful. Later on when he learned that his father was not keeping well in Pallanpur, he went back and brought him to Delhi against his wish for effective medical treatment. Gradually his father got a little used to the life in Delhi and a consolation was that he was in the company of his son. Pinki had behaved like a daughter to him and he never missed the comfort of his village. Suhanto's father spent about 18 months in Delhi and when he felt that his time has come, insisted that he may be taken back to the village. Suhanto understood this and had to relent and took him back. After about two weeks of his coming back to Delhi, Suhanto got a call from his sister that his father had passed away. He had to fly to reach on time for cremation. Pinki could not accompany because of ill health. His sister told him that his father's last words were 'I am proud of Suhanto'. Hearing this, Suhanto felt like crying. He did not shared a very open relationship with his father but he always knew that the bond was very strong. Though his father may not express but he knew that he always loved him and wanted best for him.

Also he learnt that his father had made a 'will' written and left half of his wealth to his daughter and half to Suhanto's daughter, Rupali. Suhanto made his sister the custodian of the property in the village as she lived in nearby village and can take care easily. Suhanto's sister had three sons and her husband did decent business of garments in the village and needed the property more than Suhanto. In this way two of his nephew can also make some living out of the land in Pallanpur. One of his nephew was appointed as a clerk in a health department of state government on the recommendation of Suhanto.

Mohan had also shifted to Delhi during final days of his job with 'IOU' bank and thus they both were quite in touch and spend a lot of time together. Raju also often met them as he used to travel a lot because of his business. Raju's brand 'Dharti' was the biggest name in the country in terms of sale of rice and flour products and now he had taken a back seat, allowing his sons to manage the business and he acted more as an advisor. Suhanto and Pinki occasionally made visit to America to visit their daughter. They managed to meet Khaleeq also during these visits. Only Rakesh was the one amongst the five friends who was less in the loop but he kept on writing and tried to be in touch.

Suhanto was now spending more time with himself and his family. One evening, he was sitting in the lawn of his bungalow amidst a cool evening breeze and he was reflecting on his life. He had managed to live a decent life. He was fortunate to have four good friends and a loving family. He had done quite well as a professional and he made his parents proud. This was a feeling which always eliminated the burden of responsibility and accountability on any parent or children. He was contended that his friends were all doing well and he was relieved of the responsibility he felt towards them as a friend. He was very relaxed that he had done something for the society also, apart from his contribution to charity. The biggest achievement of his life he thought was that he had struggled and came out successful from often extreme conditions and most of time he had done it with hard work and determination. He may have been unfair to someone during his life or at any point of time or may have resorted to unfair practice due to some constraints but he was contended that he had no guilt at this point of time of his life.

There was no fear of death as life was complete.